ALL ABOUT ANCIENT PEOPLES

THE VIKINGS

Anita Ganeri

ALADDIN / WATTS
London • Sydney

How to use this book

The key below shows how the subjects in this book are divided up. Included are Viking history, as well as literature, science and maths projects, geographical facts and Viking arts and crafts.

Introduction

The Vikings were sea-faring people from Scandinavia. Throughout history, they have been portrayed as fierce, brutal warriors who struck fear into the hearts of the European people. Yet, the Vikings also left an indelible mark on history as brave adventurers, shrewd traders and successful colonists. This book will help you to discover their extraordinary world.

© Aladdin Books Ltd 2009

All rights reserved

Created and produced by
Aladdin Books Ltd
PO Box 53987
London SW15 2SF

Design Omnipress Limited, UK
Designer Vivian Foster
Illustrators Peter Kesteven, David Burroughs

First published in 2009
by Franklin Watts
338 Euston Road, London NW1 3BH

Franklin Watts Australia
Level 17/207 Kent Street, Sydney, NSW 2000

Franklin Watts is a division of Hachette Children's Books, an Hachette UK company
www.hachette.co.uk

ISBN 978 0 7496 8650 5

A CIP catalogue record for this book is available from the British Library
Dewey classification: 948'.022

Printed in Malaysia

The author, Anita Ganeri (MA Cantab), has written many books for children on history, natural history and other topics.

The historical consultant, Dr Anne Millard, has written many books for children on history and archaeology.

Geography

The symbol of the planet Earth shows where geographical facts are used. These sections look at some of the routes taken by the Viking explorers, and at the lands in which they settled.

Language and literature

An open book is the sign for information on language. These sections explore how everyday words have been influenced by the Vikings. Activities include using the Runic alphabet to write a secret message.

Science and maths

The microscope symbol indicates where science information or a science or maths project is included.

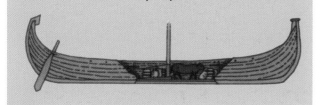

History

The scroll and the hourglass indicate where historical information is given. These sections look at key figures and events during the Viking period. They also look at the impact the Vikings had on our society today.

Social history

The symbol of a family shows where information about Viking social history is given. These sections look at the everyday lives of the Vikings.

Arts, crafts and music

This symbol gives details about the arts, crafts or musical activities of the Vikings. Projects include making Viking jewellery and creating natural dyes to colour cloth as the Vikings did.

Contents

Who Were the Vikings?

The Viking Age lasted from the end of the 8th century AD until the end of the 11th century AD. The Vikings came from Scandinavia – the present-day countries of Denmark, Sweden and Norway. The Vikings are most famous as fierce warriors, but they were also successful traders and explorers, talented poets and skilled shipbuilders and craftsmen.

One of the reasons for the Viking raids abroad was the shortage of suitable farming land in Scandinavia. Settlements were therefore mainly near the coast.

SWEDEN
Densely forested

FINLAND

NORWAY
Landscape very
mountainous

Seas and lakes
frozen in winter

Oseberg

▲ Settlements

Gotland

Oland

DENMARK
Large areas
of infertile
land

Bornmolm

In the 700s AD, the Viking population grew rapidly. Some Vikings left to seek new lands.

Hedeby

GERMANY

POLAND

Classes of society

Viking society was divided into different classes, based on wealth and land ownership. A king or chief ruled over each community. Below him were rich noblemen, or jarls (the English word 'earl' comes from this). The kings and jarls were the most powerful landowners. Below them came the freemen, or karls. They included farmers, merchants and craftsmen. At the bottom were the slaves, or thralls.

JARLS
Noblemen

KARLS
Freemen

THRALLS
Slaves

The Viking name

The Scandinavians did not call themselves Vikings. This was just a name used by early writers.

The first raid

The Viking reign of terror started with their attack on the Holy Island of Lindisfarne in June, 793 AD. They looted the monastery, killed some of the monks and carried off others to be slaves. The attack was terrifying because Lindisfarne was a holy place which they believed to be immune from attacks from the sea. The original monastery was completely destroyed by the Vikings, but was later rebuilt.

Vikings at work

Many Vikings spent time away from home on raids. They also worked as farmers, growing oats, barley, rye and vegetables. They tended cattle, pigs, sheep and goats. Fruits, such as apples, and hazelnuts and walnuts were also grown and stored for use in the winter. The Vikings hunted reindeer, rabbits, hare and wild bears. Fish were plentiful in the fjords and rivers, and the Viking fishermen caught cod, salmon and trout. Other Vikings were merchants, travelling far and wide to trade their goods. Specialist Viking craftsmen included silversmiths, blacksmiths, woodcarvers and shipbuilders.

Home Life

Family life was very important to the Vikings. The man was the head of the household. Most Viking houses only had one room in which the whole family cooked, ate and slept. They had very little furniture, and their possessions were hung around the walls. Most of the cooking was done over a fire pit in the centre. There were no windows, just a small hole to let the smoke out.

One end of the room could be divided off with a wall hanging to make a private bedroom.

Small, central hole to let the smoke out

Food and personal belongings were hung on the walls.

Loom

The head of the house had a special seat, called a high chair.

Benches around the room were used as seats and as beds.

Reeds or herbs covered the floor.

Food fit for Vikings

The Vikings ate two meals a day – breakfast and dinner. They used wooden bowls with spoons and knives, but no forks. Their diet consisted of bread with meats such as beef, mutton, seal and elk. They also ate fish, fruit, vegetables and home-made butter and cheese. They drank milk, beer or mead.

What they wore

Most Viking men wore trousers which reached to the ankle and long-sleeved shirts, or jerkins. The women wore long, loose-fitting dresses covered by two rectangular pieces of cloth, secured at the shoulders by two brooches. Clothing was mostly made of wool, but skins and furs were also used.

Children

Viking children did not go to school. Boys worked with their fathers in the fields and could go on raids when they were 16. Girls had to help their mothers at home. Family ties were very strong.

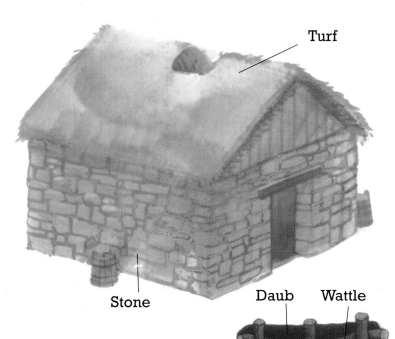

Turf

Stone

Daub   Wattle

Building materials

The Vikings built their houses out of wood or stone, with thatched roofs of straw or reeds. Turf was also used. Some houses had wattle and daub walls. The wattle was made from sticks woven together into a strong framework. This was then coated in a daub of mud, animal dung and straw to make it waterproof.

Natural dyes

Viking women often dyed their cloth with natural vegetable dyes. Try making your own using blackberries or red onion skins. Put the vegetables in a pan of water and boil it for about 3 hours (ask an adult to help you). Let the liquid cool, add your cloth and then add some salt to fix the colour. Leave it in the dye until you like the colour, then rinse in cold water.

Nature as evidence

Rubbish pits excavated at the Jorvik site in York, England, have revealed traces of animal, bird and fish bones, nutshells, eggshells and burnt pieces of grain, giving clues to the Viking diet. Soil samples also reveal what plants they grew and what kinds of insects there were.

Enlarged view of an insect's body from Jorvik

Serpents of the Sea

The Vikings are famous for their shipbuilding skills and for their longships. Their ships were among the finest built in Europe. They had different kinds of ship for each task. The best known is the longship, a canoe-shaped warship. It could withstand the stormiest seas, and yet it was shallow enough to sail up rivers and light enough to carry overland.

Evolution of boats

The earliest evidence of Scandinavian ships comes from the Bronze Age. Rock carvings show they were made from wooden frames and, it is thought, covered with ox hides. These early vessels were the forerunners of the plank-built boats of the Iron Age. The long, narrow shape of the longships first appeared in the Nydam ship of the 400s AD. The strong keel used in Viking ships was introduced in the Kvalsund Boat in the 700s AD.

Boat building

Viking ships were built from overlapping planks of oak, nailed together. Pine was used for the masts. Joints were stuffed with ropes, moss or animal hair to make them watertight.

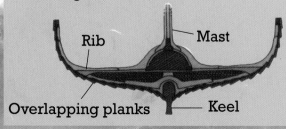

Rib — Mast

Overlapping planks — Keel

Each oarsman packed his belongings into a chest which he used as a seat while he was rowing.

Steering oar

A solid oak keel formed the backbone of the ship. The keel supported a sturdy mast and a single full sail to propel it forward at great speed when it was windy. Oars could be used in calmer weather.

Natural navigation

With no instruments or maps to use, the Vikings depended on the stars and the Sun to guide them. They also relied on land-marks and the presence of seaweed and seagulls.

By the 900s AD, the Vikings had developed a way of working out latitude (how far north), by using a table of figures, the Sun and a measuring stick.

Viking longships were often called 'Serpents of the Sea' because they had figureheads at the front carved in the shape of a fierce dragon or snake heads. The rest of the ship looked like the body of a serpent.

9

Raiders and Invaders

Driven by a shortage of land at home, the Vikings began their infamous raids in about 800 AD. Most raids were carried out by small parties of about ten boats, each carrying 30 warriors. The speed and agility of their boats meant they could surprise their enemy. At first they raided churches and monasteries for loot, but later turned their attention to towns and even began to settle in places they invaded.

The most feared Viking warriors were the berserkers. These warriors may have been drugged to make them lose control of themselves. The word 'beserk' is used today to describe a person who behaves wildly.

A Viking raid

The Viking raiders were feared throughout Europe. Imagine you are a Viking setting off on your first raid across stormy seas. How many ships are in your party? What kind of armour are you wearing? How do you plan to surprise your enemy? And how will you describe the experiences of your raid to your family and friends when you return back home?

A Viking helmet

You can make your own Viking helmet out of papier-mâché (1). Mould at least three layers of papier-mâché around an inflated balloon (2). Allow the papier-mâché to dry and burst the balloon. Trim the edges of the papier-mâché shell (3) and decorate it (4).

3

Flour and water paste

1

4

2

Balloon

Women and children

The Vikings looted and plundered the towns they raided and burned most of them to the ground. They showed no mercy to the terrified women and children. Many of them were murdered along with the men. The women were often tortured before they died. Some were taken prisoner and used or sold as slaves.

Armour and weapons

The Vikings had some of the best armour and weapons in Europe. Ordinary warriors wore tough leather tunics, while the richer ones wore chain mail. All Vikings carried a large, round shield covered in leather. They used axes, bows, spears and swords. The Viking sword was a warrior's most prized possession.

Explorers and Traders

The Vikings were not simply merciless pirates and raiders. They were also great explorers and traders. The Norwegian Vikings explored and settled in Iceland, Greenland and North America. The Danes settled in England, while the Swedes travelled to Russia and Constantinople. Merchants traded in furs, walrus ivory and farm produce for silk, silver and weapons. Thousands of coins have been found in Scandinavia. By the 10th century, Viking settlements and trading centres were widely established.

Knorrs

The Vikings used the knorr mainly for trading purposes. It was deeper and broader than the longboat. It had oars for navigating shallow waterways. Knorrs could carry a large amount of cargo.

The map below shows the Viking settlements and trade, with sailing routes marked by a solid black line. The key below shows the goods traded.

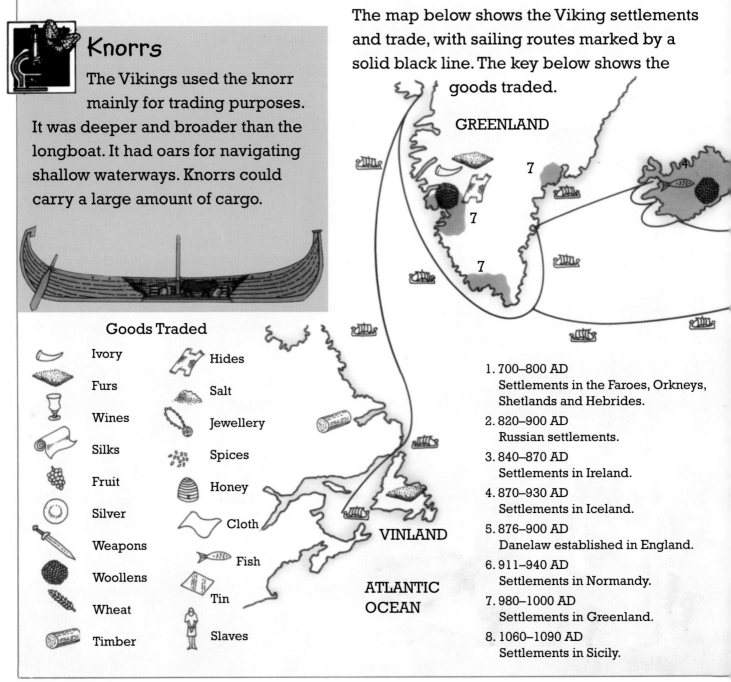

Goods Traded

Ivory

Furs

Wines

Silks

Fruit

Silver

Weapons

Woollens

Wheat

Timber

Hides

Salt

Jewellery

Spices

Honey

Cloth

Fish

Tin

Slaves

GREENLAND

VINLAND

ATLANTIC OCEAN

1. 700–800 AD
   Settlements in the Faroes, Orkneys, Shetlands and Hebrides.
2. 820–900 AD
   Russian settlements.
3. 840–870 AD
   Settlements in Ireland.
4. 870–930 AD
   Settlements in Iceland.
5. 876–900 AD
   Danelaw established in England.
6. 911–940 AD
   Settlements in Normandy.
7. 980–1000 AD
   Settlements in Greenland.
8. 1060–1090 AD
   Settlements in Sicily.

Distances travelled

The Vikings travelled great distances. For example, the journey made by Erik the Red from Iceland to Greenland was over 320 km (199 miles). If they travelled 20 km (12 miles) a day, how long would their journey have taken them? Using an atlas, plot some of the other routes and work out how long it would have taken the Vikings to get there.

False claims

Both Canada and the U.S. have claimed that the Vinland settlement was in their territory. The maple leaf, mentioned in the sagas, was adopted as a national symbol in Canada. Evidence discovered in 1962 at L'Anse aux-Meadows in Newfoundland, Canada, proved the Canadians' claims were correct.

Pick up your boat and walk

The Vikings owed much of their success in trade to their boat design. Not only could they negotiate shallow water, if they needed to go overland, they could simply pick up their boats and carry them (*see dotted lines on map*).

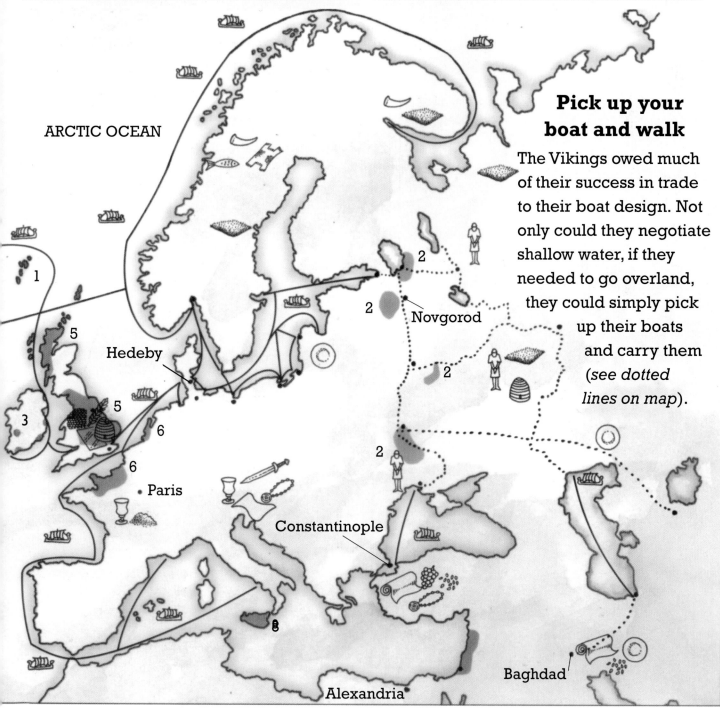

ARCTIC OCEAN

1

5

3

5

Hedeby

5

6

6

Paris

2

2

Novgorod

2

2

Constantinople

Baghdad

Alexandria

Hedeby

Hedeby in Denmark was one of the biggest and most important towns in the Viking world. It was a flourishing market town and enjoyed a key position on the major trading routes. Merchants came from as far away as France, Russia, Spain and the Middle East. Food and weapons were traded, as well as luxury items such as furs and spices. Hedeby was also an important slave market, where prisoners of war were sold to the highest bidder.

Bartering

The Vikings were great traders. Silver and gold, rare spices, silks and glass vessels were all traded in Scandinavia and abroad. To trade they needed some form of exchange. Some silver coins have been found in Hedeby, which had its own mint. Most people bought and sold with pieces of gold and silver, which were weighed on a pair of scales. Scales like the ones above have been found at Hedeby and Birka, a Viking town in Sweden.

Walrus tusks

Lead trial strip to test coin dies

Coin die

Coins

Earth ramparts

Hedeby was protected by a semi-circular rampart of earth and a sea wall of mud. It was very thick and 10 m high in places.

Viking craftsman

Archaeological evidence

In about 1050 AD, Hedeby was raided and burned to the ground by King Harald Hardrada of Norway. It never really recovered. Today only the massive earth rampart can still be seen. It was first excavated in the 1930s, and among many thousands of items found were the remains of houses and wells. One of the largest trading centres in Britain was at Jorvik (York), shown right. Archaeologists have reconstructed a Viking street from rows of shops and workhouses uncovered there.

Jewellery

The Vikings loved to wear all kinds of jewellery, including silver brooches, bracelets, necklaces and rings. Try making a piece of Viking jewellery from modelling clay. Plait together three long strands of different coloured clay. Mould four balls of clay into dragon or serpent heads for the ends. Try experimenting with some different designs.

Viking brooches

Viking ring

Viking craftsmen

Craftsmen at Hedeby included carpenters, glass blowers, silversmiths, horn carvers, leather workers, sculptors and bead makers.

Law and Order

The Vikings had no central government, legal system or police force. Each of the many communities had its own council, called the Thing. This was made up of nobles and freemen. They met regularly to settle arguments, listen to grievances, elect kings and judge criminals. Fines were the most common form of punishment. One type of fine, a *wergeld*, was paid by a murderer to his victim's family, and it had to be paid in public.

The Icelandic Althing

Iceland had its own national council, called the Althing. It first met in 930 AD and then met every midsummer. At first it had 39 chieftains, presided over by an elected Lawspeaker. The Althing lasted for two weeks and was a great social event. Today, Iceland's parliament is still called the Althing. The parliament on the Isle of Man meets every summer on the site of the island's Viking Thing.

Isle of Man flag

Thingvellir, the site of the Althing, in Iceland

Havamal

In addition to the laws agreed at the Althing, the Vikings also had a series of sayings relating to everyday life. The Havamal was compiled in the 9th century, and offered advice such as: *Be a friend to your friend, match gift with gift; meet smiles with smiles, and lies with dissimulation.*

Women's rights

Viking women were allowed to own land and other property, and a wife had the right to share in her husband's wealth. Women could divorce and act as farmers and traders. They were also expected to defend the homestead.

Jonsbok

At first Viking laws were not written down, but passed on from one generation to the next by word of mouth. The ancient code of Icelandic laws can be found inscribed in vellum (calfskin) in the Jonsbok. The illustration here comes from a 16th century copy of the Jonsbok.

The Holmganga duel

The Holmganga duel had very strict rules. It was fought on a piece of cloth 3 m (3.2 yd) square. If either man stepped off the cloth, he was considered a coward.

At the end of the duel, the man with the most sword wounds had to pay his opponent in silver. If he died the victor won his property.

Viking Burials

When a Viking died, he or she might be buried or cremated in a ship or in the ground. This depended on the individual's position in society and on their wealth. Viking funerals were times of great ceremony. Vikings believed in life after death, so dead people were buried with their personal belongings to take to the next world. Huge cemeteries and burial mounds have been found at towns such as Jelling in Denmark.

A middle-class burial

Middle-class Vikings were buried in wooden chambers, with personal belongings and food and drink for their journey.

Barrel of milk

Spindles

Comb

Viking master buried with slave (Thrall)

Horses

Site evidence

Most of the evidence about the Vikings and their ships comes from the grave mounds. Two of the finest Viking ships, from Gokstad and Oseberg (see pages 26–27), were uncovered as ship burials. If the family could not afford a ship burial, then stones in the shape of a ship were placed around the burial site.

Funeral pyre (right)
The Vikings believed if a body was burnt, his spirit would go to Valhalla (see page 20).

Modern day festivals

Every year, on the last Tuesday of January, the people of Lerwick in Shetland relive their Viking history. They celebrate Up-Helly-Aa, a modern version of a Viking fire festival. A model of a longboat is pulled through the town by a torchlit procession, which includes a 'jarl' and his band of Viking warriors. The ship is set alight to represent a funeral pyre of a Viking chieftain. This is followed by all-night feasting and singing.

Dead man's hunting dog and possessions

Broken shield

Bent sword

Spear

Sacrifices

An Arab trader called Ibn Fadlan told the fascinating story of the cremation of an important Viking chieftain. A young slave woman from the chieftain's household was chosen to die with her master. A ship was drawn up onto the land and surrounded with firewood. It was then filled with the chieftain's prized possessions and his body was put on a couch. The young servant girl lay by her master's side and was sacrificed by an old woman called the 'Angel of Death'. She was 'a stout and grim figure' who was in charge of such rituals. A relative of the dead man then stepped from the crowd, naked, and set the boat ablaze with a torch.

Angel of Death

Gods and Religion

Until their conversion to Christianity in the 10th and 11th centuries, the Vikings worshipped many gods. The most important were Odin, Thor and Frey. Odin was the chief god and the god of battle. He ruled Asgard – the home of the gods. Thor was the god of thunder and lightning. He rode across the sky in a mighty chariot, wielding his huge hammer, Mjollnir.

Days of the week

Some days of the week are named after Viking gods. Tuesday is named after Tyr, the god of war. Wednesday comes from Woden, or Odin. Thursday comes from Thor's day and Frigga's day (Friday) from Frigga, the wife of Odin.

Valhalla

Valhalla was the hall in Asgard to which the Viking warriors slain in battle were sent. They were called the Einheriar. They were led to Asgard by the Valkyries, beautiful young women sent by Odin. Each day in Asgard, the Einheriar would do battle and each night they would be brought back to life.

Njord was the god of the sea and the father of the twins, Frey and Freya.

Freya was a fertility goddess and also goddess of beauty, love, war and death. She was Frey's twin sister.

Frey was god of fertility and of summer.

Loki

Balder

Loki and Balder
Loki was the god of lies and mischief. He tricked the god Hoder into killing his brother, Balder. Loki was jealous of Balder's beauty and popularity.

Asgard

Asgard was the home of the gods. It was invisible to the human eye as it floated above Earth. It was separated from Earth by a river, called Ifing.

Ragnarok

Viking mythology was concerned with life after death and what would happen if all the gods were killed. Ragnarok was to be the final battle between the forces of good and evil, between the gods and the giants and monsters. Odin, Thor and Frey, among others, would die. Others would survive and build a new and better world.

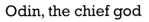

Odin, the chief god

Types of worship

In 950 AD, another Arab traveller called Ibrahim al-Tartushi visited Hedeby. In the story of his travels, he describes a ritual followed by a citizen who had made a sacrifice to the gods. The body of the sacrificed animal – either an ox, a ram, a goat or a pig – was put onto poles outside the door of his house. In this way, his neighbours learned of his pious deed.

Thor, the god of thunder

Language and Literature

The Vikings were great poets and storytellers. They told tales of great heroes, warriors and battles. These stories were called sagas. The Viking alphabet consisted of 16 characters, called runes. Each rune was made up of straight lines so that it could be carved into wood or stone. The sagas were written down by scholars in the 13th century using Latin not runes.

The scene on the right is one of several carved into wood at Hylestad church in Norway. The scenes depict Sigurd, a Viking hero, testing the blade of his sword. The blade snaps and Regin, the blacksmith, has to forge another one. Sigurd later uses the new blade to kill a dragon who is guarding some treasure.

A B C D E F G H I K L M

A secret code

The runic alphabet, or *futhark*, was invented about 2,000 years ago. Runes were associated with magic and were often used as a kind of secret code for charms or curses. Write your own message using the Runic alphabet shown above. Can you work out what is written here?

22

Writing it down

The Viking sagas were first written down in the 13th century on vellum (calfskin). Sharpened quill feathers from swans or ravens were used as pens, and a glossy ink was distilled from berries. This picture is an extract from *Flateyjarbok*, depicting the death of St Olaf at Strikesland.

The runic stone above can be found by a roadside near Broby, in Sweden.

Runes in literature

Many writers have invented languages based on runes. In *The Hobbit*, the author J R R Tolkien uses magical runes as the alphabet of the dwarves. They used it to mark secret doors, write secret instructions and keep secret records.

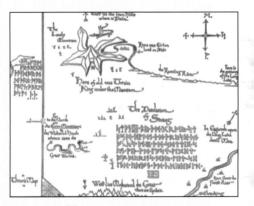

N O P Q R S T U V W X Y Z

Naming places

As the Vikings settled in new lands, they often gave the places Viking names. Many of these names survive today. For example, Milford in Wales came from the Viking words *melr* (meaning sandbank) and fjord. Other Viking names include the words dale (valley), kirk (church) and beck (brook or stream). The town of Schleswig in Germany comes from the term *vik-place*, which means a place where the Vikings went raiding or trading. Some surnames also reflect Viking influences. For example, Nott, comes from the great Viking chief, Canute. Can you think of any other Viking names which survive today?

The Danes

The Vikings can be roughly divided into three groups according to where they came from. On their raids, the Danes mainly went to England, France, Germany and Spain. They invaded England in 865 AD and ruled in the east of the country until 1042. This area became known as Danelaw. King Alfred the Great of Wessex stopped them spreading westwards.

The map shows Denmark at the time of the Vikings. Denmark today consists of the Jutland peninsula, two large islands and almost 500 smaller islands. In Viking times it also included part of southern Sweden. In the south the Viking frontier was defended by a huge earth rampart, the Danevirke.

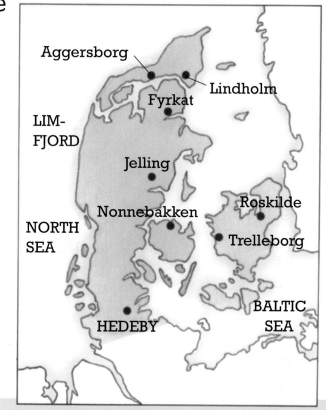

Aggersborg
Lindholm
Fyrkat
LIM-FJORD
Jelling
Roskilde
Nonnebakken
NORTH SEA
Trelleborg
BALTIC SEA
HEDEBY

Lindholm Høje

Linholm Høje is one of the greatest Viking burial grounds to be found in Scandinavia. Most of the graves contained cremations dating from 500 AD onwards. Around 800 AD, the stones around the graves were set in the shape of ships, illustrating that the Vikings believed the ship to be the symbol of the journey into the afterworld. A town was also discovered near the cemetery. The picture here is part of the elaborately carved portal from the Norwegian stave-church at Urnes.

24

The Jelling stone

The Jelling stone was set up at Jelling in Demark in the 980s AD by King Harald Bluetooth, as a memorial to his parents who were buried there.

Kings of Denmark

For much of the Viking Age, Denmark did not have one overall king. For a time it was ruled by kings from Sweden. Then in the 930s or 940s, Gorm the Old became king and united Denmark. He was succeeded by his son Harald Bluetooth, who ruled until 986 AD. Harald was overthrown by his own son, Swein Forkbeard. Forkbeard's son, Canute, ruled over Denmark, Norway and England from 1014–1035 AD.

Harald Bluetooth

Feasts and festivals

All Vikings loved festivals, and huge feasts were held for Viking men coming home after a raid. At these feasts, families were reunited, gossip was exchanged and weddings were arranged. There were three major feasts each year – one after Christmas, the second in April and the third at the end of October to celebrate the gathering of the harvest.

Games

Dice games and pegboard games were popular among the Vikings, as were games such as draughts and chess. In the evenings, Viking children would sit around the fire and make up short poems, like limericks, stories and riddles.

A Viking chess board

Kingy bats was played with a bat and ball.

The Norwegians

The Norwegians began their raids with an attack on Lindisfarne in 793 AD. After raiding many places in Europe, they turned their attention to the North Atlantic. In the late 800s the first group of Vikings went to Iceland. In 1000 AD, Leif Erikson, son of Erik the Red, led a party to North America. They landed in Newfoundland, Canada, which they later called Vinland, because so many wine-making grapes grew there.

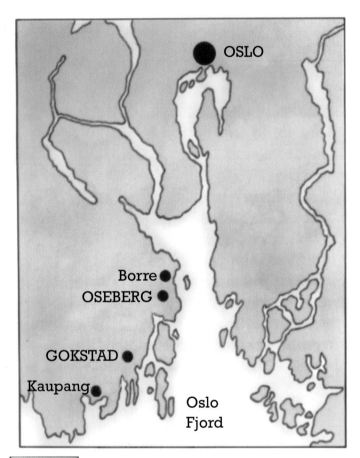

OSLO

Borre
OSEBERG

GOKSTAD

Kaupang

Oslo
Fjord

The Gokstad and Oseberg ships

In 1893, a reconstruction of a 9th-century Viking ship found at Gokstad sailed  across the Atlantic Ocean from Norway to Newfoundland, Canada. This proved that the Vikings could have reached North America long before Columbus. Another famous ship, the 9th-century Oseberg burial ship, was found in 1904. It contained the skeletons of a queen and her servant. Both ships are now on display at a museum near Oslo, Norway.

Erik the Red and Greenland

After banishment from Norway for murder, Erik the Red settled with his family in Iceland. In 982 AD he was exiled again. He set sail for an even harsher island. He called it Greenland, in the hope that other people would go to live there. Eventually there were about 3,000 Norwegian settlers in Greenland. Life was tough due to the climate, but the settlements lasted for about 500 years.

Burial wagon

Competitions

Games that prepared the participants for battle were extremely popular among the Vikings. The games included wrestling, swimming, fencing, boulder-throwing and archery. The Vikings' favourite pastime, however, was horse-fighting, for which stallions were specially bred.

Boulder-throwing (left) and horse-fighting (right)

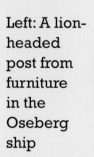

Left: A lion-headed post from furniture in the Oseberg ship

A detail from the cradle of the wagon shown below, left

A beautifully carved prow from the Oseberg ship

Kings of Norway

The Norwegian royal family are descendants of Harald Fine Hair. Hakon I claimed the throne in 935 AD until he was killed in battle in 960 AD. Olaf Tryggvason reigned until 1000 AD. The Danish king, Swein Forkbeard took power until his death, then his son Canute and St Olaf II became rivals for the throne. Canute defeated his rival at the Battle of Stiklestad in 1030 AD. Later kings were Magnus, Harald Hardrada, Magnus II and Olaf III.

An illustration from Harald Fine Hair's Saga in the *Heimskringla*

The Swedes

In the early 800s, Swedish Vikings sent raiding parties up the rivers into Russia. They were called 'Rus' by the Slavic people. They also raided Constantinople (now Istanbul), and traded with merchants from Persia. The Swedes were converted to Christianity in the 11th century under the reign of King Olaf Skottkonung.

Uppsala

Uppsala in Sweden was the site of one of the most notorious pagan cult centres in Scandinavia. In 1075 AD, a German cleric called Adam of Bremen wrote about a festival which took place every nine years. He wrote of sacrifices being carried out in a sacred grove next to a pagan temple. Nine heads of each kind of male creature, both human and animal, were offered to the gods. There was also a large tree, at the base of which was a well where the human sacrifices were made. If the victim sank, they believed he had been accepted by the gods.

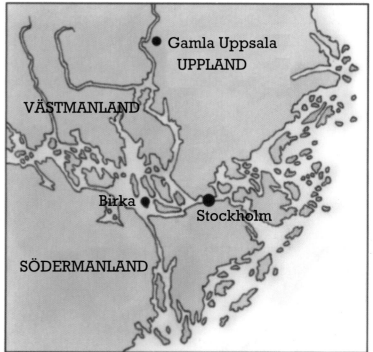

The map above shows Sweden during the Viking Age. They needed to find suitable land for their growing population. Their raids were for both trading and setting up colonies.

Winter activities

During the long months of the harsh Scandinavian winter, Viking men used to repair their tools and forge new weapons. There was also skating, skiing and sledging and, of course, snowball fights. Viking skates uncovered at Jorvik were made from animal bones. One side of the bone was polished flat for sliding over ice.

Skates were attached to shoes with leather ties. Long poles were used to push skaters over the snow.

Gotland

Gotland is an island in the Baltic Sea, off the east coast of Sweden. It was at the centre of the Viking trade routes and, as a result, became wealthy and thriving. Thousands of Viking artefacts have been found at Gotland. They include 400 carved picture stones, which show ships and warriors being welcomed to Valhalla.

Russia and beyond

The Viking's chief interest in the East was trade. In the 860s AD, three brothers were asked by the Slavs 'to restore order and to rule over them'. This land became known as 'the land of the Rus', from which the name Russia comes. Swedish Vikings also acted as bodyguards to the Byzantine Emperor. They were known as the Varangian Guard.

One of the oldest crucifixes found in Scandinavia

The decline of the Vikings

In 1066, at the Battle of Stamford Bridge, the Norwegian king, Harald Hadrada, was killed trying to conquer the English. Hedeby was also destroyed that year by Polish tribesmen. Many of the Viking raiders started to settle in their chosen lands, and little by little the terrifying raids and invasions ceased. The Bayeux tapestry (right) records the Norman invasion of England by William the Conqueror, a descendant of the Viking chief, Rollo.

789 AD Viking ships off England.

793 Lindisfarne, Iona and Jarrow raided.

795 Viking raid near Dublin.

835 Start of 30 years of raiding on England, Germany and France.

c.860 Iceland discovered. National monarchies established in Norway, Sweden and Denmark.

862 Vikings begin trading in Russia.

866 Danish kingdom established at York. Vikings control English Danelaw.

872–930 Norwegians settle in the Orkneys and Shetlands.

875–900 Colonisation of Iceland.

911 Vikings granted control of Normandy.

934 Germans capture Hedeby.

c.965 Harald Bluetooth and Hakon the Good become Christians.

986 Erik the Red settles Greenland.

985–986 Viking explorers sight America (Vinland).

1017–1035 Reign of Canute the Great.

1066 English defeat Norwegians at Stamford Bridge. Normans defeat English at Hastings.

8000 BC

First hieroglyphs (picture writing) in Egypt c.3500 BC

Old Kingdom in Egypt 2686–2150 BC

Pyramids built in Egypt during Old Kingdom

Egyptian Middle Kingdom 2040–1640 BC

2000 BC

Reign of Tutankhamun – the boy pharoah 1347–1339 BC

New Kingdom in Egypt 1552–1085 BC

Romulus and Remus found the city of Rome 753 BC

500 BC Roman Empire c.27 BC– AD 476

Julius Caesar murdered 44 BC

Fall of the Roman Empire AD 476

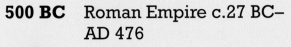

Viking raids across western Europe AD 793–1000

AD 1000 First Crusade to recapture Holy Land from Muslims AD 1096

First mechanical clock AD 1386

The Aztec Empire in Central America AD 1300s–1521

AD c.1200 –1532 The Inca Empire in South America

First cities – Jericho and Catal Hüyük 8000–5650 BC

Wheel invented by the Sumerians 3500–3000 BC

Rise of the Indus Valley civilisation 2500–1700 BC

Early Minoan period in Crete begins c.2500 BC

Stonehenge completed in England c.1500 BC

Destruction of Knossos in Crete. End of the Minoan period c.1400 BC

Shang Dynasty in China c.1766–1122 BC

Siddhartha Gautama, the Buddha c.500 BC

Birth of Confucius 551 BC

The Golden Age of Greece 479–431 BC

Alexander the Great conquers Persia, Syria and Egypt 333–330 BC

The Qin dynasty in China 221–206 BC

The Great Wall of China completed in 214 BC

Samurai warriors of Japan 1100s–1850 AD

The Plague, or Black Death, spreads in Europe AD 1300s.

First mechanical printing press developed by Gutenberg in Germany in AD 1450.

Christopher Columbus sets sail for the West Indies and discovers America AD 1492.

Glossary

Althing The national council of Iceland.

Asgard The home of the Viking gods.

Beserkers The most feared Viking warriors.

Danelaw The area of eastern England ruled by the Danish Vikings.

Einheriar Name given to Viking warriors killed in battle.

Jarls Rich noblemen and landowners in Viking society.

Karls Freemen in Viking society, including farmers, merchants and craftsmen.

Ragnarok The final battle between the Viking gods and the forces of evil.

Runes The characters, or symbols, which made up the Viking alphabet.

Rus The name given to Swedish Vikings who travelled to trade in the area now called Russia.

Saga Story about Viking battles.

Skalds Court poets.

Thing Viking council.

Thralls Viking slaves.

Valhalla A hall in Asgard for warriors killed in battle.

Index

Photographic credits:

Abbreviations: t=top, m=middle, b=bottom, r=right, l=left

All pictures were supplied by CM Dixon Photo Resources apart from: 9, 11t all, 12t, 14t, 20t – Roger Vlitos. 4 – Stockbyte. 5 – Spectrum. 6–7 all, 8, 15t, 15mr, 18t, 19, 22t, 24t, 25m, 28b – York Archaeological Trust. 16 all, 24m, 26t – Frank Spooner Pictures. 17 – Institute of Copenhagen. 20b, 21, 29b – Mary Evans. 23t, 27br – by kind permission of the Manuscript Institute of Iceland. 23b – illustrated by JRR Tolkien with permission of Grafton Books, an imprint of HarperCollins Publisher Ltd. 26m, 26b, 27t – University of Oslo.